Starry

the *Tiny,* Shiny Star

Kristine Angela

Illustrations by Alissa Dicke - Editor Jason Ring

Art work @ Alissa Dicke

www.starrythestar.com

ISBN

979-8-8693-5373-3

Kristine Angela is an accomplished author, actress, and voice-over artist from Chicago, Illinois, now residing in Los Angeles, California.

She is thrilled to present her second book to you. Her first book, "Cuppy the Special Cupcake," has been loved by children of all ages.

"Starry the Tiny, Shiny Star" is a charming story about the star we wish upon. It is a heartwarming tale about the longing to be noticed and what can happen when you truly believe in yourself. The story emphasizes the idea that by helping just one person, we can make a positive impact on the entire world.

Alissa was born a storyteller. Growing up in Utah she spent countless hours drawing, singing, dancing, and acting.

After almost a decade pursuing acting in Los Angeles, CA she moved to Florida's Treasure Coast with her husband to raise their two children.

Reading with her kids reignited her love of children's books and the power they can have for developing minds. She hopes to bring joy through her illustrations.

Many lifetimes ago, high up in the night sky, floated a tiny glowing star.

She was known as Starry.

Alone and patiently in deep thought, this tiny star wondered what her purpose was.

While gazing out into the vastness of space, Starry decided that she wanted to be the most noticed star in the galaxy. And so, she developed a plan.

"When all my friends go to bed, I will remain bright and awake. I will shine my light down on Earth and hope to catch the attentior of the children below," Starry declared.

That night, Starry waited until everyone else had gone to sleep. She twinkled and radiated brighter than ever before.

Unfortunately for her, another star had the same idea, a much bigger and even brighter star.

Down below, a little boy named Joseph was scanning the night sky from his bedroom window. He searched for the brightest star he could see to make his wish to.

Joseph saw Starry faintly twinkling. But then he noticed that big star and Joseph made his wish to him instead.

The big star soon became everyone's favorite in the kingdom of stars.

All of the dimmer stars gathered around him and cheered!

Feeling discouraged, Starry cried out, "ENOUGH! I will twinkle with all of my might even if just one person notices me."

The next night everyone went to bed except for Starry.

Starry noticed Amelia, a seven-year-old girl who appeared to be upset.

Amelia felt sad because her older brother and sister teased her earlier that day. She clung to her brown curly hair as her pillowcase caught all her cascading tears.

Amelia was up way past her bedtime!

But before going to sleep, she made sure to say her goodnight prayers to the moon and the sky.

"Goodnight moon, goodnight sky. Bless mommy and daddy and please don't let my brother and sister pick on me tomorrow," Amelia sobbed.

At that moment, Starry, the tiny star emerged out of the darkness and into the little girl's world.

Amelia's tears stopped upon realizing that someone had listened to her for the first time.

She was filled with an overwhelming gush of joy.

Amelia beamed with excitement!

She pointed up and shouted, "I have my very own twinkling star in the pretty sky!"

There was no more darkness, but rather a bright path of light that filled her room.

From that moment on, little Amelia never felt alone again.

Every night before going to sleep, Amelia says her goodnight prayers to the moon, the sky, and her new friend Starry the tiny, shiny star.

All this joy came from one tiny star, who felt invisible until a little girl discovered her.

The next day, the other stars praised Starry for her desire and hard work. Starry was someone they looked up to. She was now their new friend.

That is when Starry had a realization. "I am just as special as everyone else even though I'm tiny," she squealed with a burst of excitement.

The tiny star now realized that she had the power to dry the eyes of the children below.

She would give them a hug from the sky by bathing them in her comforting glow.

Starry became the star that we say goodnight to.

And the star that we wish upon.

But most importantly, she is the star that never leaves our side.

Not only does she appear every night in the darkness, but if you look closely during the day, you might just spot this tiny, shiny star.

Only those who truly believe will be able to find her.

Starry didn't need to prove to the others that she was the biggest or brightest in the universe.

She only had to believe in herself.

When you look past the exterior we are all tiny, shiny stars waiting to be noticed.

The End.

Kristine's 1st Grade Poem (1991)
(Inspired by her teacher Mrs. Krushing and Dr. Seuss)

"Reading is My Life"

I love reading.
I love it so much, I want to
read every day of my life.
I can read.
You can read.
Everyone can read, if they try.
I love reading so, so much.
I read to my Mother.
I read to my Brother.
I read to my Father, and
I read to my Grandma,
even on the phone!
I read in the car.
I read near and far.
So as you can see
I still read to my
Mother, Father and Brother,
wherever they are.
So as you can see,
I love reading.
I love it so much.
I hope you do too!

Milton Keynes UK
Ingram Content Group UK Ltd.
UKHW050023300524
443259UK00001B/2